Aberdeenshi•
c~

Countries Around the World

Algeria

Lori McManus

www.raintreepublishers.co.uk
Visit our website to find out
more information about
Raintree books.

To order:
☎ Phone 0845 6044371
🖺 Fax +44 (0) 1865 312263
🖂 Email myorders@raintreepublishers.co.uk

Customers from outside the UK please telephone +44 1865 312262

Raintree is an imprint of Capstone Global Library Limited, a
company incorporated in England and Wales having its registered
office at 7 Pilgrim Street, London, EC4V 6LB – Registered company
number: 6695582

Text © Capstone Global Library Limited 2012
First published in hardback in 2012
The moral rights of the proprietor have been asserted.

Edited by Abby Colich and Megan Cotugno
Designed by Philippa Jenkins
Original illustrations © Capstone Global Library Ltd 2012
Illustrated by Oxford Designers & Illustrators
Picture research by Liz Alexander
Originated by Capstone Global Library Ltd
Printed in China by CTPS

ISBN 978 1 406 23561 6 (hardback)
16 15 14 13 12
10 9 8 7 6 5 4 3 2 1

British Library Cataloguing in Publication Data
McManus, Lori.
    Algeria. -- (Countries around the world)
    965'.054-dc22
A full catalogue record for this book is available from the British
Library.

Acknowledgements
We would like to thank the following for permission to
reproduce photographs: Alamy: pp. 15 (© imagebroker), 30 (© vario
images GmbH & Co.KG), 31 (© Robert Harding Picture Library
Ltd); Corbis: pp. 7 bottom (© Owen Franken), 25 (© Dani Cardona/
Reuters), 35 (© Pascal Parrot/Sygma); Dreamstime.com: pp. 7
top (© Carolecastelli), 20 (© Dmitry Pichugin), 26 main (© Paul
Maguire), 32 (© Santamaradona); Getty Images: pp. 8 (Apic/Hulton
Archive), 9 (SuperStock), 10 (Keystone-France/Gamma-Keystone),
22 (Pascal Le Segretain), 23 (Farouk Batiche/AFP), 28 (© 2009
PKG Photography), 29 (Fayez Nureldine/AFP); iStockphoto: pp. 13
(Michel Gunther), 16 (Jean-Paul Garcin), 18 (Alain Dragesco-Joffé),
21 (Michel Gunther); Shutterstock: pp. 5 (© 46 (© margusson).

Cover photograph of sand dunes in Tassili n'Ajjer, Tuareg, Algeria,
reproduced with permission from Photolibrary (Ismadl Schwartz).

We would like to thank Shiera S. el-Malik for her invaluable help in
the preparation of this book.

Every effort has been made to contact copyright holders of material
reproduced in this book. Any omissions will be rectified in
subsequent printings if notice is given to the publisher.

Disclaimer
All the internet addresses (URLs) given in this book were valid at
the time of going to press. However, due to the dynamic nature of
the internet, some addresses may have changed, or sites may have
changed or ceased to exist since publication. While the author
and publisher regret any inconvenience this may cause readers, no
responsibility for any such changes can be accepted by either the
author or the publisher.

Contents

Introducing Algeria...4

History: struggle for independence and peace...........................6

Regions and resources: mostly desert 12

Wildlife: from boars to flamingos 18

Infrastructure: seeking stability...22

Culture: life together 28

Algeria today...34

Fact file 36

Timeline 40

Glossary 42

Find out more 44

Topic tools 46

Index 48

Some words are printed in bold, **like this**. You can find out what they mean by looking in the glossary.

Introducing Algeria

Have you ever read about or seen pictures of Algeria? What do you know about this large African country? If you imagine a vast, hot, desert landscape, you are on the right track. About four times the size of Spain, Algeria's land is over 80 per cent desert. The Sahara Desert covers most of North Africa, including Algeria and its neighbouring countries.

However, very few Algerians live in the sun-baked desert. Algeria also has a beautiful coastline where the land meets the Mediterranean Sea. Most Algerians live near this coast. Here, farms are abundant and large cities have modern services such as satellite television and access to the internet.

Although people have lived in the region since ancient times, Algeria was established as an independent country just 50 years ago. Since its **independence**, Algeria has had problems such as unhealthy water, too few houses, and even civil war. In this same period of time, the country has made strong progress in providing education and healthcare to its people. Algeria's government has also become a leader for peace and **trade** in North Africa.

In the midst of both problems and growth, Algeria's people maintain strong traditions. Family ties are very important. Religious beliefs guide everyday actions as well as major decisions. Music expresses wise sayings, religious ideas, and strong emotions. With a rich history and deep values, Algerians are proud of their land and **heritage**.

Recent unrest

Recently, Algeria has experienced **unrest** in its cities. In early 2011, groups of angry Algerians gathered to publicly complain about high food prices, lack of freedoms, and dishonesty among leaders. Many Algerians hope the unrest will lead to positive changes in the government.

It is easy to get lost in Algeria. The Sahara Desert covers much of the country. The Sahara, the world's largest desert, covers 8.6 million square kilometres (3.3 million square miles) of Africa.

History: struggle for independence and peace

Algeria's long history is marked by invasions. As a result, its boundaries have changed many times. Algeria finally gained **independence** in 1962. For the last 50 years, the country has experienced **unrest** because of conflicts over government and religion.

The original people

The first **inhabitants** in the region of Algeria were called **Berbers**. The Berbers were herders and hunters. Over time, the Sahara Desert expanded over the grassy herding areas. The Berbers gradually moved north to the mountains and coastal region near the Mediterranean Sea.

Ancient conquerors

Around 1100 BC, the first non-Berber people settled in North Africa. These people came from Phoenicia, an ancient land now known as Lebanon. The Phoenicians **subdued** the Berbers, taking many of them as slaves. The conquerors built towns along the coast so they could **trade** goods with others by way of the sea.

In the 800s BC, the Algerian region came under the control of Carthage, an ancient trading city. Many Berbers were trained to fight in the Carthaginian army. Over the next 600 years, the Berbers sometimes fought for Carthage and sometimes fought for another empire based in the city of Rome.

Rome defeated Carthage and took over North Africa in 105 BC. The Romans established farms that produced grains, grapes, beans, and olive oil. The Romans also brought Christianity to the region. Christianity became the religion of about 30 per cent of the people.

The ancient Romans built roads and aqueducts in the lands they invaded. Remains of these structures still exist in Algeria.

Some Berbers stayed in the mountain regions of Algeria through the invasions. These Berbers preserved a unique, ancient language and culture.

More invasions and the arrival of Islam

Over time, the Roman Empire weakened. The Vandals, a fierce tribe from Germany, invaded Roman-occupied North Africa in AD 429. Troops from the Byzantine Empire then defeated the Vandals in AD 534.

In the 600s, **Arab** armies invaded North Africa. The Arabs brought the religion of **Islam** with them. Over the next 600 years, most Berbers adopted Islam and the Arab culture. Berbers and Arabs often married each other. Arabic became the shared language across North Africa.

The Ottoman Empire

In the early 1500s, Christian troops from Spain captured Algeria's coastal cities. The Berber rulers feared that their Islamic way of life would end. They asked for help from the **Muslim** Ottoman Empire. The Ottomans, based in present-day Turkey, pushed the Spanish Christians out of North Africa.

As a result, Ottoman governors called *deys* ruled Algeria from the 1500s to the early 1800s. The *deys* allowed the Berber tribes in the mountains to govern themselves. They also allowed North African pirates to attack and demand money from European traders in the Mediterranean Sea. The pirates gave a portion of their money to the *deys*.

In 1529, Khayr al-Din led the capture of Algiers for the Ottoman Empire. Europeans nicknamed him "Barbarossa," which means "red beard" in Italian.

EL-HADJI-ABD-EL-KADER.

French invasion

The pirates' reign ended in 1830 when France invaded the city of Algiers. The French then expanded their power to the mountain areas. In 1848, Algeria officially became a part of France, and Algeria's modern borders were established.

Guided by Muslim leader Abd al-Qadir, many Arabs and Berbers fought fiercely against French control.

Colonial rule

France encouraged Europeans to move to Algeria. The Europeans received free or low-cost land to farm. Often, Muslim families had to move to cities or less **fertile** land as a result. Under French rule, Muslim Algerians could not serve in the government or even vote.

Struggle for independence

In 1954, the Algerian National Liberation Front (FLN) started a violent **revolt** against the French government. The French fought back by burning homes and farms. After eight years of fighting, Algeria declared independence from France on 5 July 1962.

In a demonstration for independence, Algerians confront the French army.

Internal struggles

The new government made decisions that helped a few, but not all, Algerians. Many Algerians remained poor. By the mid-1980s, many Algerians were angry with the government. **Riots** broke out across the country in 1988.

In response, the government allowed more than one **political party** to take part in elections. The Islamic Salvation Front (FIS) wanted to make Algeria a country ruled by **sharia**, or laws based on the Muslim holy book, the **Koran**. To stop this from happening, the military took action.

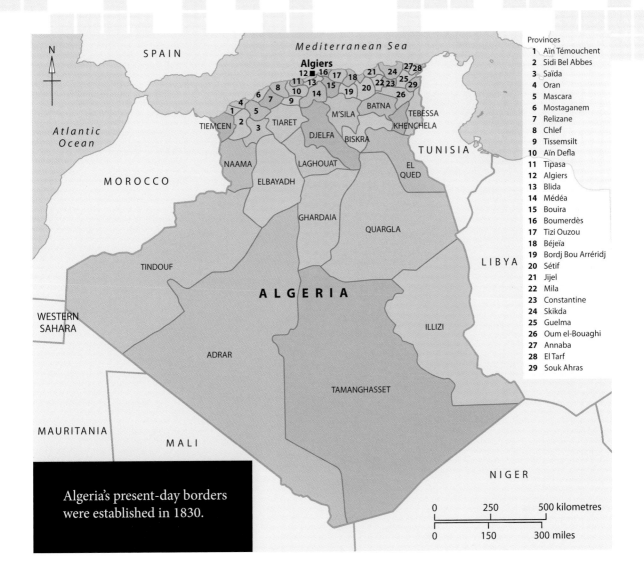

SPAIN

Mediterranean Sea

Algiers
12 ■ 16
11 13
6 7 8
4 5
1
2 3

Provinces
1 Aïn Témouchent
2 Sidi Bel Abbes
3 Saïda
4 Oran
5 Mascara
6 Mostaganem
7 Relizane
8 Chlef
9 Tissemsilt
10 Aïn Defla
11 Tipasa
12 Algiers
13 Blida
14 Médéa
15 Bouira
16 Boumerdès
17 Tizi Ouzou
18 Béjeïa
19 Bordj Bou Arréridj
20 Sétif
21 Jijel
22 Mila
23 Constantine
24 Skikda
25 Guelma
26 Oum el-Bouaghi
27 Annaba
28 El Tarf
29 Souk Ahras

Atlantic Ocean

MOROCCO

TIEMCEN

NAAMA

ELBAYADH

TIARET

M'SILA

DJELFA

BISKRA

LAGHOUAT

BATNA

TEBESSA

KHENCHELA

TUNISIA

EL QUED

GHARDAIA

QUARGLA

LIBYA

TINDOUF

A L G E R I A

ILLIZI

WESTERN SAHARA

MAURITANIA

ADRAR

M A L I

TAMANGHASSET

N I G E R

Algeria's present-day borders were established in 1830.

0   250   500 kilometres

0   150   300 miles

A seven-year civil war erupted between the military-backed government and the FIS. Factories, bridges, railways, and other buildings were purposefully damaged during the war. An estimated 100,000 people died.

In 1999, with the support of the military, Abdelaziz Bouteflika was **elected** president. Violence decreased as a result of Bouteflika's effort to work with the **mullahs**, the Muslim religious leaders. However, recent **protests** produced conflicts with police and showed that some Algerians remain angry with the government.

Regions and resources: mostly desert

Algeria is situated in northern Africa along the Mediterranean Sea. It is one of the largest countries in Africa. The Tellian Atlas Mountains and the Saharan Atlas Mountains cross Algeria from east to west. These mountain ranges divide the country into three zones, or regions.

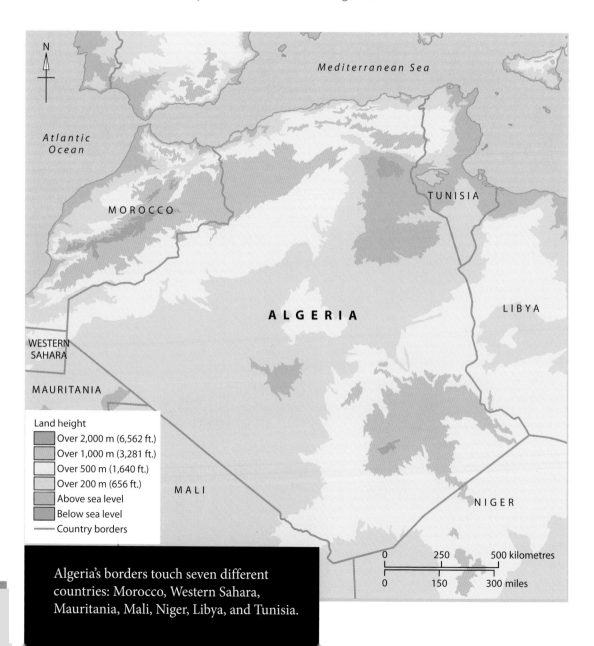

Land height
- Over 2,000 m (6,562 ft.)
- Over 1,000 m (3,281 ft.)
- Over 500 m (1,640 ft.)
- Over 200 m (656 ft.)
- Above sea level
- Below sea level
- Country borders

Algeria's borders touch seven different countries: Morocco, Western Sahara, Mauritania, Mali, Niger, Libya, and Tunisia.

Algeria's northern border spans the Mediterranean Sea. The coastline is beautiful, but rough.

The coastal zone

Between the Tellian Atlas Mountains and the Mediterranean Sea lies a narrow, hilly coastal zone. The land here is **fertile**. The mild climate makes this region, called the Tell (the Algerian word for "hill"), good for **agriculture**. Summers are hot and dry; winters are mild and wet. Algeria's few rivers twist among these hills and valleys.

The Tell is home to 90 per cent of the Algerian population. Major cities such as Algiers, Oran, and Constantine are scattered along the Mediterranean coast. Severe earthquakes shake this region regularly. Floods and mudslides can also present problems during the rainy winters.

Daily life

In the spring and summer, a hot, dry wind called the **sirocco** blows north across the Sahara Desert. The wind picks up sand as it travels. When it reaches the coastal region, the sirocco coats everything with a thin film of dust. The dust can make it difficult to breathe. Most Algerians wear scarves to protect their faces. When the sirocco is blowing, it can be difficult to see more than 30 metres (100 feet) ahead.

High plateaus

Between the Tellian Atlas and Saharan Atlas mountain ranges is a high **plateau** region. This area averages an elevation (height) of 914 metres (3,000 feet) above sea level. With limited rainfall and high winds, the land is dry and rough. Still, the plateaus are home to over 3 million Algerians. These Algerians farm sheep, cattle, goats, and barley to survive.

The Sahara Desert

South of the Saharan Atlas Mountains, the Sahara Desert covers the rest of Algeria. The temperature here during the day can reach 49ºC (120ºF) and then drop to near freezing at night. Certain sections of the desert go without rain for up to 20 years. The sand dunes are usually between 2 and 5 metres (7 and 16 feet) high, but some are taller than palm trees!

Although the Sahara Desert takes up 80 per cent of Algeria's land, only 3 per cent of the population lives here. Most of these 1.5 million people are **nomads** or semi-settled **Bedouin**, desert-dwelling **Arab** tribes. However, some Algerians live permanently in **oases** where water from beneath the ground reaches the surface.

Daily life

The Tuareg **Berbers** have made their home in the Sahara Desert for thousands of years. Today, Tuaregs **trade** camels, breed cattle, and create objects from metal. They produce beautiful swords, jewellery, and metal crafts. When travelling by camel, Tuaregs use saddles that make the ride more comfortable and also provide storage space.

The Sahara Desert contains more than just sand. Rock cliffs, large stones, and gravel are found at Mount Tahat, Algeria's highest point.

Oil **refineries** and pipelines are common in Algeria's desert.

Natural energy resources

Algeria's desert is not a welcoming place to live. However, large **reserves** of oil and natural gas lie under the ground. Oil was first discovered in Algeria in 1956. Since that time, the oil and gas **industries** have provided wealth for Algeria. More than 95 per cent of money earned through **exporting** comes from these **resources**.

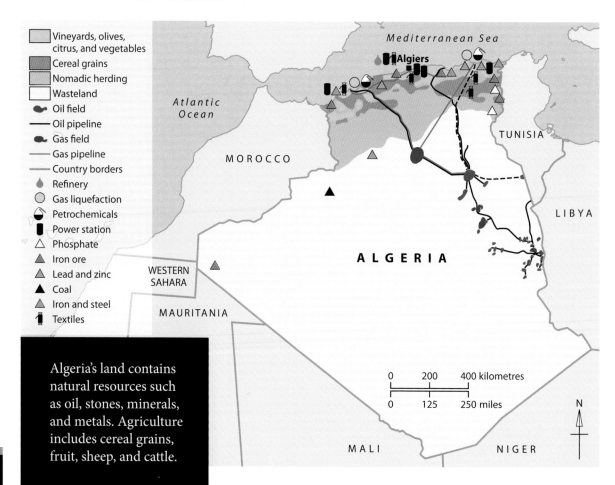

Vineyards, olives, citrus, and vegetables
Cereal grains
Nomadic herding
Wasteland
Oil field
Oil pipeline
Gas field
Gas pipeline
Country borders
Refinery
Gas liquefaction
Petrochemicals
Power station
Phosphate
Iron ore
Lead and zinc
Coal
Iron and steel
Textiles

Mediterranean Sea
Algiers
Atlantic Ocean
TUNISIA
MOROCCO
LIBYA
ALGERIA
WESTERN SAHARA
MAURITANIA
0   200   400 kilometres
0   125   250 miles
N
MALI   NIGER

Algeria's land contains natural resources such as oil, stones, minerals, and metals. Agriculture includes cereal grains, fruit, sheep, and cattle.

The mining industry

Besides oil and gas, Algeria has other important resources under the ground. Minerals such as iron, lead, zinc, and copper are continually **mined** from Algerian land. Phosphate, a mineral used in fertilizer, has been mined since 1891. Algerians also mine salt, gold, cement, and valuable stones such as **onyx** and marble.

Factories and farms

Manufacturing is another important industry in Algeria. The most common products made in the factories are steel, **textiles**, and construction materials. Factories also process food and electricity.

Agriculture provides jobs for 14 per cent of the Algerian population. Most farms are located in the Tell where the soil is **fertile**. Algerians grow cereal grains such as rye, wheat, barley, and oats. Fruits such as figs, grapes, citrus, and olives are also common crops. Sheep are reared for their wool and meat, while cattle are bred for dairy products and meat.

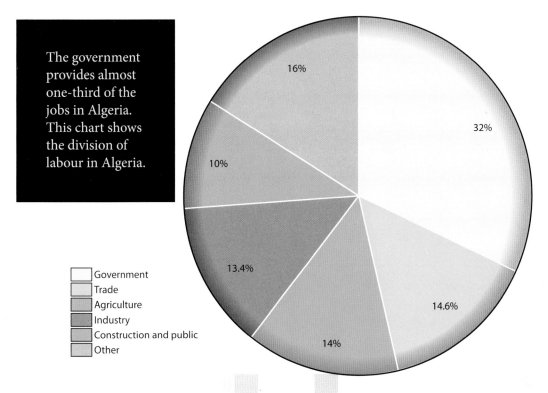

The government provides almost one-third of the jobs in Algeria. This chart shows the division of labour in Algeria.

- Government
- Trade
- Agriculture
- Industry
- Construction and public
- Other

16%
32%
10%
13.4%
14.6%
14%

Wildlife: from boars to flamingos

The abundant wildlife in Algeria includes monkeys, deer, porcupines, eagles, snakes, and even marine mammals. Algerians are working to protect wild animals and places of natural beauty in their country. However, water pollution harms the animals and the people.

Mammals

Wild boars, jackals, and hares are some of the most common land animals in Algeria. The fennec fox and the sand cat live in the desert regions. The thick fur on the bottom of the sand cat's feet provides protection from the extreme desert temperatures. The fennec fox's large ears allow it to hear prey from far away.

Golden jackals are common in Algeria. They have large ears and long, bushy tails. Jackals hunt birds, rodents, and young gazelles in dry, open areas.

Flamingos wade in Algeria's salt marshes. Using their long beaks, the birds can strain small bits of food out of the mud.

Birds and other creatures

Flamingos, pintail ducks, and several varieties of geese find food in Algeria's **salt marshes**. Algeria is also home to raptors such as vultures, golden eagles, and hawks. Born elsewhere, the northern bald ibis flies to Algeria to live in the western Sahara. Snakes, monitor lizards, and scorpions live throughout the **semi-arid** regions. Algeria also has many insects, some of which cause problems. The bites of mosquitoes can pass along a disease called **malaria**.

Endangered species

Algeria's most **endangered** animal is the Barbary serval. This wild cat has large ears, long legs, and spots like a leopard. The Mediterranean monk seal lives off the coast of Algeria and other Mediterranean countries. This seal is considered one of the world's most endangered species.

National parks

Algeria has many national parks. The land and animals in these parks are protected so that Algerians can enjoy them both now and in the future. The parks cover a variety of **ecosystems**, including the coast, desert, and mountains.

Gouraya National Park has beautiful beaches as well as tall cliffs. The park includes the waters of the Mediterranean Sea near the coast. Marine mammals such as the harbour porpoise, bottlenose dolphin, and sperm whale find protection here.

Djurdjura National Park is located in a mountainous region in northern Algeria. This area is known for its thick forests, unusual caves, and beautiful lakes. The park is home to a variety of animals, including the red fox, weasel, and peregrine falcon. The endangered Barbary macque, a type of monkey, also lives in Djurdjura National Park.

Tassili n'Ajjer National Park contains sandstone cliffs and arches. Scientists believe rock paintings in the park are 7,000 years old.

Water pollution

Many Algerians want to keep their land and water clean. However, some **industries** dump **sewage** and oil waste into rivers and the Mediterranean Sea. Soil and fertilizer from farms also wash into the waterways. Many Algerian people and animals do not have clean water to drink.

Chemicals and waste collect in rivers and streams in Algeria. The pollution makes the water unsafe to drink.

How to say...

Arabic, the official language of Algeria, is written with an alphabet different from the Roman alphabet. The Arabic words below have been written with the Roman alphabet so that you can pronounce them.

falcon	*ajdal*	**desert**	*badiya*
forest	*haraj*	**cave**	*ghar*
monkey	*hibn*	**mountain**	*jabal*
whale	*hut*	**sea**	*bakhr*

Infrastructure: seeking stability

Algeria is making progress toward **stability**. Recent government decisions have helped settle conflicts and provide important services. Like many other nations, Algeria experiences problems in **urban** areas due to **unemployment** and a lack of housing.

A republic

Algeria is officially called the People's Democratic Republic of Algeria. This highlights the fact that Algeria is a **republic**, a type of government in which the people choose their leaders. The head of the government is the president. The president serves a five-year term, but can be re-**elected** many times.

Algeria has a **parliament** chosen by the voters and the president. This group makes laws, but the president has more power than the parliament.

ABDELAZIZ BOUTEFLIKA

(B.1937)

Abdelaziz Bouteflika is Algeria's current president. As a young man, Bouteflika was an officer in Algeria's National Liberation Army. Then, from 1963 to 1979, he served as the foreign minister. Bouteflika was first elected president of Algeria in 1999. He was re-elected in 2004 and 2009.

Abdelaziz Bouteflika has been re-elected twice and could run for president again in 2014.

Protests for change

Some Algerians distrust the government. In early 2011, groups of angry Algerians protested against high food prices and poor management by leaders. As a result, President Bouteflika promised changes, such as a fairer election system and a new plan to improve the **economy**.

Leader in North Africa

Algeria has helped other African countries to solve conflicts. In 2006, Algeria helped create a peace agreement in the neighbouring country of Mali. In 2009, Algeria led other North African nations in a new plan to stop **terrorism**. Algeria belongs to several international organizations that support **trade**, peace, Islamic causes, and protection of the environment.

Education

Algerians value education. The education system has grown tremendously since the country's **independence** in 1962. Before independence, fewer than 10 per cent of Algerians could read and write. Now the **literacy rate** is about 70 per cent.

Literacy rates	
Female	60.1%
Male	79.6%
Total population	69.9%

Algeria provides free education to all children. Schooling is required for nine years, from age 6 to 16. Pupils must pass a national exam to get into secondary school. They also compete against each other for places at universities or technical colleges.

Because the majority of Algerians are under the age of 20, schools tend to be crowded. In some cities, children go to school in shifts – one group in the morning, and a different group in the afternoon.

Algerian primary school children learn maths, Arabic, history, science, and the fundamentals of **Islam**. Some study French, starting in Year 4. Children learn to write both the Roman alphabet as well as the traditional, flowing Arabic script.

How to say...

book	*kitab*	student	*daris*
school	*madrasa*	mathematics	*rayadi*
history	*tarikh*	university	*jami'a*

YOUNG PEOPLE

Algerian children do not have to wear a uniform in school. In fact, they often wear comfortable clothing such as jeans and T-shirts. However, pupils must dress **modestly**. Lunch is eaten at school. The government provides a school lunch for children of families with little money.

Algerian children attend school for about six hours per day. The school day starts around 8.00 a.m.

Urban life

Over half of all Algerians now live in urban areas. Many **rural** families move to cities in search of work, but there are not enough jobs for everyone. There are not enough places to live, either. Algeria is currently short of 1.5 million homes, even after large construction projects in the 1990s.

Slums have developed on the outskirts of Algeria's cities as a result of housing shortages and unemployment. These neighbourhoods are overcrowded, run-down, and often dirty and unhealthy. Some of these areas lack basic services such as clean drinking water, electricity, or waste disposal.

Population of major cities in Algeria	
Algiers	2,900,000
Oran	1,170,000
Constantine	808,000
Annaba	350,000

Healthcare

The Algerian government provides free basic medical care through a system of clinics and hospitals. Algerians enjoy better health conditions than most people in Africa. Still, the number of doctors, nurses, and dentists is small compared to the number of Algerians who need healthcare.

Currency

The dinar is the official **currency** in Algeria. Dinars were introduced in 1964 after independence from France. Algerians use dinars in the form of coins and bills.

Pictures of important buildings, animals, and locations are printed on Algerian money.

Many Algerians live in apartment blocks. It is typical for nine people to live together in a three-bedroomed apartment.

Daily life

Algerians who need to travel within the country usually drive cars or trucks. Most of the major roads are paved, except in the southern Sahara region. Some people who live in the desert still travel by camel.

Culture: life together

Algerians are proud of their land and culture. Traditions are important, and family is the foundation of society. Many Algerians express their identities and feelings through art, including literature and music.

The people

Ninety-nine per cent of Algerians are **Arab**, **Berber**, or mixed Arab-Berber. Sometimes Berbers and Arabs clash because of differences in language and power in government.

Arabic is the official language of Algeria. However, Berbers speak Tamazight, a language that was recognized by the government only in 2002. French is widely understood in Algeria and used in media, education, and government.

Daily life

Algerian men often gather at coffee shops or cafés to play chess, draughts, cards, or dominoes. Although women sometimes join them, they are more likely to socialize at home.

Muslim prayers are said five times daily.

After Algeria's independence, more women began to attend university and take professional jobs. These women are newly graduated police officers.

Religion

Both Berbers and Arabs follow **Islam**, Algeria's main religion. Followers of Islam are called **Muslims**, and the vast majority of Algerians are **Sunni** Muslims. Muslims believe their holy book, the **Koran**, contains the words of God as told to the Prophet Muhammad.

Role of women

Typically, an Algerian woman marries the man her father chooses for her. In traditional families, women rarely have jobs outside the home. Most Algerian women cover their faces in public, according to traditional Islamic custom.

During the war for **independence**, some Algerian women actively fought alongside the men. Since then, more and more women have enrolled at universities and colleges and obtained jobs. Today, 60 per cent of university students are women.

Literature

Algeria has produced many great writers and thinkers. Mohammed Dib (1920–2003) wrote more than 30 novels as well as poems, short stories, and books for children. Many of Dib's later books are set during the war for independence from France.

Albert Camus (1913–1960) was born in Algeria. The son of a French colonialist, Camus wrote many influential novels and essays. He won the 1957 Nobel Prize for Literature.

ASSIA DJEBAR

(B. 1936)

Algeria's most famous living writer is Assia Djebar. She is a professor of history at the University of Algiers. Her novels and short stories focus on the difficulties faced by women in North Africa. Djebar is also an award-winning filmmaker.

Music

Music has always been important in Algerian society. Poetry with lively musical accompaniment preserves Algeria's rich folklore. Called *rai* (pronounced "rye"), the **lyrics** can include wise advice, historical lessons, and religious values.

Some think of modern *rai* music as "rebel" music. The songs tell about problems in cities and in government. The beat is easy to dance to, mixing rock, jazz, and hip-hop with traditional Arabic sounds. Algerian Cheb Khaled, born in 1960, became a *rai* superstar in North Africa and Western Europe during the 1990s.

Men wearing long robes and turbans sing poetry and play instruments. The beat is vibrant, even a bit wild.

YOUNG PEOPLE

Young Algerians often turn to music as a means of expressing their frustrations. One of these frustrations is **unemployment**. Half of all Algerians under the age of 30 do not have regular jobs. Many young people joined the **protests** in early 2011 to voice their anger. At least 500 students gathered to complain about a new law that decreased the importance of a university degree.

Sports

Football is the most popular sport in Algeria. Across the country, people play football in stadiums, empty fields, and school grounds. Algerians also enjoy boxing, wrestling, tennis, running, swimming, and skiing. In the desert areas, camel racing is a favourite sport.

Football is played all over Algeria.

Media

Satellite television is popular in Algeria. Many watch both European and Arab channels. Algerians have access to a variety of newspapers and radio stations. The government controls most media sources, yet there is more freedom of speech than in other North African countries.

Algeria's major cities have internet access. In 2008, 4.1 million Algerians were using the internet, mostly in cybercafés or with dial-up connections. Mobile phones are now quite common, especially amongst young people.

Food

Algerians enjoy meals with family and friends. The traditional Arabic flatbread, called *khabz*, is an Algerian **staple**. Algerians eat lamb, beef, and fish. Meals usually include vegetables and are flavoured with dried red chilies, black pepper, cumin, and other spices.

Coclo (Big Meatballs)

Coclo is enjoyed by many Algerians. Ask an adult to help you make this recipe.

Ingredients

- 450 g minced beef
- 140 g rice
- 1 clove of garlic, finely chopped
- 1 medium egg, beaten
- ½ teaspoon salt
- ½ teaspoon ground bayleaf
- ⅛ teaspoon ground mace
- ¼ teaspoon pepper
- ⅛ teaspoon thyme
- 2 tablespoons olive oil
- 1 medium onion, finely chopped
- ½ bunch of coriander leaves, tied in a bundle
- 175 ml water

Method

1. Mix the beef, rice, garlic, egg, salt, bay leaf, mace, pepper, thyme, and olive oil together well. Shape into two large meatballs.
2. Put onion, coriander, and water in a pan. Add meatballs. Cover the pan and simmer over low heat for 2 hours or a bit more.
3. Discard the coriander. Serve the meatballs with rice or couscous.

Serves 6

Algeria today

After years of turmoil and violence, Algeria is making strides toward peace and **stability**. In the last 50 years, the **economy** has benefited from oil and gas discoveries. Now all Algerian children have access to school. Security in the cities has improved through active police presence and safety measures.

Yet Algeria's cities remain overcrowded, with too many people and too few jobs. In early 2011, **protests** broke out in Algeria over **unemployment** and the high prices of food. Two people were killed in conflicts with police. In response, the government promised changes to improve the economy. Some Algerians question the government's ability or honest desire to help the common people.

Militant Islamic groups have also increased public attacks and bombings since 2006. These groups do not want the Algerian government to join with other countries to fight **terrorism**. Instead, they want the Algerian government to be led more strongly by **sharia**.

Despite the continuing conflicts, Algerians remain committed to their families, their culture, and their beliefs. Algerians are known to be warm and welcoming to friends and neighbours. They enjoy sharing food, sports and games, and lively conversation.

The strong people and natural **resources** of Algeria provide the building blocks for a stable nation. With more pubic services, job opportunities, and honesty in government, Algerians can look forward to a good future in their beautiful, rugged land.

Algerians are very hospitable. A popular Algerian saying expresses this kindness toward visitors: "When you come to our house, it is we who are the guests, for this is your house."

Fact file

Country name: People's Democratic Republic of Algeria

Capital: Algiers

Languages: Arabic (national and official language), Tamazight (national language), French

Religions: Sunni Muslim (official religion): 99%
Christian or Jewish: 1%

Ethnic groups: Arab-Berber: 99%
European: less than 1%

Type of government: Republic

Independence date: 5 July 1962

National anthem: "Qassaman" (We Pledge) was written during the struggle for independence from France in the mid-1900s.

We swear by the lightning that destroys,
By the streams of generous blood being shed,
By the bright flags that wave,
Flying proudly on the high mountains,
That we are in revolt, whether to live or to die,
We are determined that Algeria should live,
So be our witness, be our witness, be our witness!

We are soldiers in revolt for truth
And we have fought for our independence.
When we spoke, nobody listened to us,
So we have taken the noise of gunpowder as our rhythm
And the sound of machine guns as our melody,
We are determined that Algeria should live,
So be our witness, be our witness, be our witness!

Population:	34,586,184 (est. 2010)
Life expectancy:	74.26 years
Currency:	Algerian dinar
Bordering countries:	Morocco, Western Sahara, Mauritania, Mali, Niger, Libya, and Tunisia
Total land area:	2,381,741 square kilometres (919,595 square miles)
Largest cities:	Algiers, Oran, Constantine, Annaba
Terrain:	mostly high plateau and desert; coastal plain bordered by mountains
Climate:	arid to semi-arid; mild, wet winters with hot, dry summers along coast; drier with cold winters and hot summers on high plateaus; the sirocco is a hot, dust- and sand-laden wind especially common in summer
Highest elevation:	Mount Tahat: 3,003 metres (9,852 feet)
Lowest elevation:	Chott Melrhir: 40 metres (131 feet) below sea level
Coastline:	998 kilometres (620 miles)
Major rivers:	Chelif River, Seybouse River
Major landforms:	Chott Melrhir (salt flat), Guelma springs (limestone cones), Sebkha Azzel-Matti (lake), Mount Tahat, Grotte Karstique de Ghar Boumaaza (underground cave network)

Natural resources:	petroleum, natural gas, iron ore, phosphates, uranium, lead, zinc
Industries:	petroleum, natural gas, light industries, mining, electrical, petrochemical, food processing
Agricultural products:	wheat, barley, oats, grapes, olives, citrus, fruit, sheep, cattle

National holidays:

1 January	New Year's Day
1 May	Labour Day
19 June	National Day
5 July	Independence Day
1 November	Anniversary of the Revolution

Famous Algerians:

St Augustine (AD 354–430), writer and philosopher

Abdelkader Alloula (1929–1994), playwright

Ahmed Ben Bella (b. 1918), Algeria's first president

Hassiba Boulmerka (b. 1968), Olympic runner

Albert Camus (1913–1960), writer

Sidi Bu Madyan (1126–1198), Islamic mystic, Algeria's patron saint

Hamid Cheriet (b. 1949), musician

Cheb Mami (b. 1966), singer

Abd al-Qadir (1808–1883), resistance fighter against the French

Workers on farms make up 14 per cent of the work force in Algeria.

Timeline

BC is short for Before Christ. BC is added after a date and means that the date occurred before the birth of Jesus Christ (for example, 450 BC).

AD is short for Anno Domini. AD is added after a date unless the date is spelled out or it refers to whole centuries. It means that the date occurred after the birth of Jesus Christ (for example, AD 720).

BC

around 3000	First Berber groups settle in what is now Algeria.
1100s	Phoenicians occupy the coastal region of North Africa.
800s	Algerian region comes under the control of Carthage.

AD

100s	Rome defeats Carthage and takes over North Africa.
429	Vandals gain control of North Africa.
534	Byzantine troops defeat the Vandals.
600s	Arabs invade North Africa and bring Islam to the region.
700s	Algeria becomes part of the Islamic Empire.
1000–1235	Several powerful Berber kingdoms dominate North Africa.
1200–1500	Berber kingdoms decline; Arabs from Egypt and the Middle East settle in North Africa.
1505–1511	Spain establishes forts along the Algerian coast.
1514–1529	Ottoman Turks help push the Spanish Christians out of Algeria.
1530–1830	Algiers is ruled by Ottoman governors.
1830	France takes control of Algiers.

1848	Algeria becomes part of France.
1912–1918	Algerians help France during World War I.
1939–1945	Algerians fight to defend France against Germany in World War II.
1954	Algerians begin to revolt against France.
1962	Algeria gains independence from France.
1980	An earthquake in El Asnam kills approximately 5,000 people.
1988	Protests break out in cities due to high food prices and lack of services; constitution is revised to allow more than one political party in elections.
1990	Government declares a state of emergency and cancels election results when it seems that FIS party will win.
1992–1999	Civil war breaks out between the military-backed government and conservative Islamic militants; more than 100,000 people die.
1999	Abdelaziz Bouteflika elected president; major fighting ends.
2002	Tamazight (Berber language) declared a national language.
2007	Terrorist attacks against government buildings kill over 80 people.
2009	Bouteflika is elected to third term as president.
2011	Protests over high food prices and unemployment erupt in Algiers.

Glossary

agriculture farming; the production of crops or livestock

Arab member of an Arabic-speaking people

Bedouin Arab of the desert in Asia or Africa

Berber member of a group of native North African tribes

currency money

dey title of the Ottoman governor of Algiers before the French took over in 1830

economy management of the resources, finances, income and expenses of a community or country

ecosystem collection of living things and the environment in which they live

elect choose by voting

endangered in danger of becoming extinct

export ship to other countries for sale

fertile (regarding land) capable of abundant plant growth

heritage anything that has been handed down from the past or by tradition

independence freedom from the control of others

industry organized business activity concerned with making, mining, processing, or constructing materials

inhabitant person or animal that lives in a place

Islam religious faith of Muslims, based on the Koran and teachings of the prophet Muhammad

Koran holy book of Islam, believed by Muslims to be the word of God

literacy rate percentage of people over the age of 15 who can read and write

lyrics words of a song

malaria illness with chills and fever caused by the bite of an infected mosquito

manufacturing making of goods by people or machines

militant extremely aggressive

mine remove metals, rocks, or minerals from the ground

modest not showing too much of a person's body

mullah title of respect for a religious leader who teaches and studies the Koran

Muslim follower of the religion of Islam

nomad member of a tribe who has no permanent home, but moves from place to place

oasis (pl. oases) green area in a desert region, usually with a natural water supply

onyx variety of stone with alternating white and black bands

parliament assembly of people who make laws for a country

plateau level area of land raised above the land around it

political party organization that seeks to influence the government

protest organized public demonstration of disapproval

refinery factory where raw materials such as oil, metal, or sugar are made pure

republic form of government in which the people elect their leaders

reserve something kept or stored for use

resource source of wealth in a country, such as precious metal, fertile land, or oil

revolt rebellion against leaders or government

riot noisy, violent public fight caused by a crowd of people

rural related to living in the countryside

salt marsh area of low, flat land that is frequently flooded by salt water

semi-arid having little yearly rainfall

sewage waste matter carried in water away from a community

sharia laws based on the Koran that outline the duties and penalties for Muslims

sirocco hot, dry, dusty wind blowing from North Africa across the Mediterranean Sea

slum dirty, run-down place to live

Sunni Muslim one of two main branches of Islam; the other is Shiite

stability steady and lasting

staple basic or necessary item of food

subdue overpower by force

terrorism regular use of violence or threats to achieve a goal

textile any fabric or cloth

trade process of selling, buying, or exchanging goods between countries

unemployment not having a regular job

unrest state of being troubled or uneasy

urban relating to a city or town

Find out more

Books

Africa (Facts At Your Fingertips), Derek Hall (Wayland, 2008)

Algeria, Falaq Kaqda (Marshall Cavendish, 2009)

Algeria in Pictures, Francesca Davis Dipiazza
  (Twenty-First Century Books, 2008)

Deserts (Geography Fact Files), Katie Powell (Ed.) (Wayland, 2007)

The Story of Islam (Usborne Young Reading: Series Three), Rob Lloyd Jones
  (E.D.C. Publishing, 2007)

Websites

www.bbc.co.uk/learningzone/clips/living-without-water-algerian-foggara-s/11950.html
Find out about the communities that are springing up in the desert regions of Algeria, and the ancient methods that humans are using to find underground water.

travel.nationalgeographic.com/travel/countries/algeria-photos
View interesting photos and maps of Algeria on the National Geographic site.

Places to visit

Jamaa el Kebir Mosque, Oran
The oldest mosque in Algiers, the Jamaa el Kebir (Great Mosque) was originally built in the 1000s AD.

Martyr's Monument, Algiers
This enormous concrete structure was built to remember people who lost their lives during the Algerian war for independence from France (1954–1962).

Palace of Ahmed Bey, Constantine
Hajj Ahmed built this beautiful palace after he became the governor (*dey*) of Constantine in 1826. The palace contains 250 marble columns, plus many courtyards filled with gardens and fruit orchards.

Grand Erg Oriental, Saharan Lowlands
This spectacular "field of sand dunes" in the Sahara Desert covers a large area of northeastern Algeria.

Tassili n'Ajjer National Park, Djanet
View beautiful sandstone cliffs and arches as well as prehistoric cave paintings at this national park in the Sahara Desert.

Further research

Which topics in this book caught your interest? Do you want to learn more about life in the Sahara Desert? Do you want to listen to Algerian *rai* music? Would you like to see a photograph of the Barbary serval? Visit your local library to check out books, DVDs, CDs, or magazines to help you learn more about Algeria.

Topic tools

You can use these topic tools for your school projects. Trace the map on to a sheet of paper, using the thick black outline to guide you.

The Algerian flag is half green and half white. The colour green represents Islam. The colour white stands for purity and peace. The red crescent and star in the middle are symbols of Islam. The colour red represents liberty.

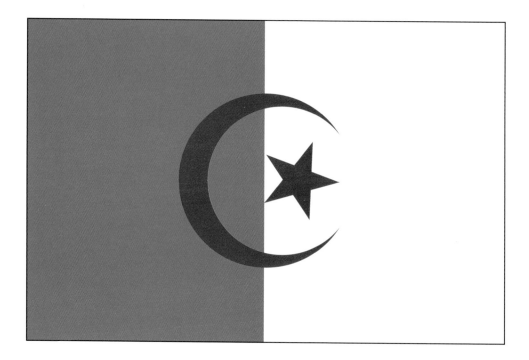

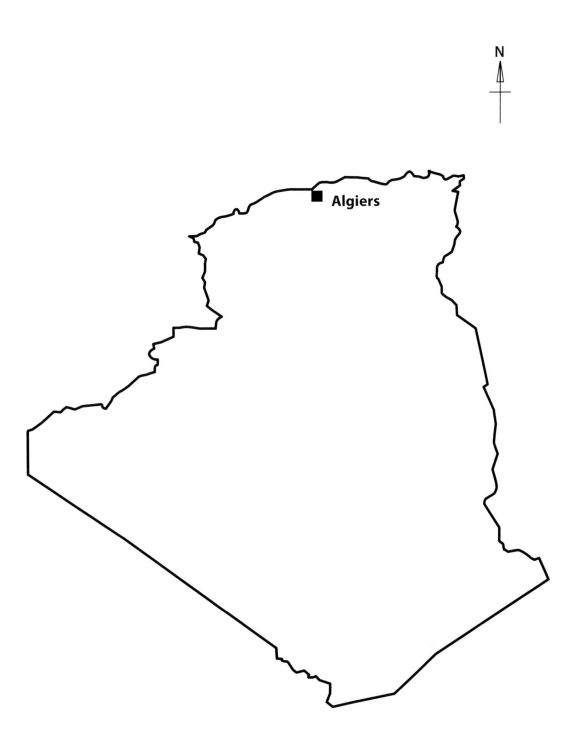

N

Algiers

Index

Algiers 9, 13, 26, 30
animals 14, 17, 18, 19, 20, 21, 32
Arabs 8, 9, 14, 28, 29

Barbary macques 20
Barbary servals 19
Bedouins 14
Berbers 6, 8, 14, 28, 29
birds 19
borders 6, 9
Bouteflika, Abdelaziz 11, 22
Byzantine Empire 8

Camus, Albert 30
Carthaginians 6
Christianity 6, 8
cities 4, 8, 9, 10, 13, 24, 26, 30, 32, 34
civil war 4, 11
climate 13, 14
clothing 25, 29
coastline 4, 6, 8, 13, 19, 20
coclo (meatballs) 33
coffee shops 28
communications 32
Constantine 13, 26
crops 17
currency 26

deserts 4, 6, 13, 14, 16, 18, 19, 20, 27, 32
deys (Ottoman governors) 8
Dib, Mohammed 30
dinars (currency) 26
diseases 19
Djebar, Assia 30
Djurdjura National Park 20
dust storms 13

earthquakes 13
economy 26, 34
education 4, 24, 25, 28, 29
elections 10, 11, 22
endangered species 19, 20
exports 16

families 4, 10, 25, 26, 28, 29, 32, 34
farming 4, 6, 10, 13, 17, 21

fennec foxes 18
flooding 13
foods 17, 25, 32, 33, 34
football 32
France 9, 10, 26, 30

Gouraya National Park 20
government 4, 6, 10–11, 22, 25, 26, 28, 30, 32, 34

healthcare 4, 26
houses 4, 10, 22, 26, 28

independence 4, 6, 10, 24, 26, 29, 30
insects 19
internet 4, 32
Islamic religion 8, 11, 23, 24, 29, 34
Islamic Salvation Front (FIS) 11

jobs 17, 22, 26, 29, 31, 34

Khaled, Cheb 30
Koran (holy book) 10, 29

land area 4
languages 8, 21, 24, 28
laws 11, 22
literacy rate 24
literature 30
livestock 14, 17

Mali 23
manufacturing 17
marine life 20
marriage 8, 29
media 28, 32
Mediterranean monk seals 19
Mediterranean Sea 4, 6, 8, 12, 13, 19, 20, 21
mining 17
mobile phones 32
music 4, 30, 31
Muslims 8, 10, 11, 29

National Liberation Front (FLN) 10, 22
national parks 20
natural gas 16, 34

oases 14
oil reserves 16, 34
Oran 13, 26
Ottoman Empire 8

parliament 22
Phoenicians 6
phosphate 17
pirates 8, 9
plateau region 14
political parties 10
pollution 18, 21
population 13, 14, 26
presidents 11, 22
protests 11, 23, 31, 34

rai (music) 30
recipe 33
religious beliefs 4, 6, 8, 11, 23, 24, 29, 30, 34
riots 10
Roman Empire 6, 8

Sahara Desert 4, 6, 13, 14, 16, 18, 19, 20, 27, 32
Saharan Atlas Mountains 12
salt marshes 19
sand cats 18
sharia (Islamic law) 11, 34
sirocco winds 13
slums 26
sports 32, 34

television 4, 32
Tellian Atlas Mountains 12
Tell region 13, 17
terrorism 23, 34
trade 4, 6, 8, 14, 23
transport 14, 27
Tuaregs 14

unemployment 22, 26, 31, 34

Vandals 8

water 4, 14, 18, 20, 21, 26
women 28, 29, 30

Titles in the series

Afghanistan	978 1 406 22778 9	Japan	978 1 406 23548 7
Algeria	978 1 406 23561 6	Latvia	978 1 406 22795 6
Australia	978 1 406 23533 3	Liberia	978 1 406 23563 0
Brazil	978 1 406 22785 7	Libya	978 1 406 23564 7
Canada	978 1 406 23534 0	Lithuania	978 1 406 22796 3
Chile	978 1 406 22786 4	Mexico	978 1 406 22790 1
China	978 1 406 23547 0	Morocco	978 1 406 23565 4
Costa Rica	978 1 406 22787 1	New Zealand	978 1 406 23536 4
Cuba	978 1 406 22788 8	North Korea	978 1 406 23549 4
Czech Republic	978 1 406 22792 5	Pakistan	978 1 406 22782 6
Egypt	978 1 406 23562 3	Philippines	978 1 406 23550 0
England	978 1 406 22799 4	Poland	978 1 406 22797 0
Estonia	978 1 406 22793 2	Portugal	978 1 406 23578 4
France	978 1 406 22800 7	Russia	978 1 406 23579 1
Germany	978 1 406 22801 4	Scotland	978 1 406 22803 8
Greece	978 1 406 23575 3	South Africa	978 1 406 23537 1
Haiti	978 1 406 22789 5	South Korea	978 1 406 23551 7
Hungary	978 1 406 22794 9	Spain	978 1 406 23580 7
Iceland	978 1 406 23576 0	Tunisia	978 1 406 23566 1
India	978 1 406 22779 6	United States of America	978 1 406 23538 8
Iran	978 1 406 22780 2	Vietnam	978 1 406 23552 4
Iraq	978 1 406 22781 9	Wales	978 1 406 22804 5
Ireland	978 1 406 23577 7	Yemen	978 1 406 22783 3
Israel	978 1 406 23535 7		
Italy	978 1 406 22802 1		